In Celebration of;

_____

_____

Date: _____

Guest Name

_____

_____

_____

Messages & Wishes

_____

_____

_____

_____

_____

_____

_____

_____

_____

_____

_____

Guest Name

Memories & Wishes

Guest Name

Messages & Wishes

Guest Name

Memories & Wishes

_____

_____

_____

_____

_____

_____

_____

_____

_____

_____

_____

_____

_____

_____

_____

Guest Name

Messages & Wishes

Guest Name

Memories & Wishes

Guest Name

Messages & Wishes

Guest Name

Memories & Wishes

Guest Name

Messages & Wishes

Guest Name

Memories & Wishes

Guest Name

Messages & Wishes

Guest Name

Memories & Wishes

Guest Name

Messages & Wishes

Guest Name

Memories & Wishes

Guest Name

Messages & Wishes

Guest Name

Memories & Wishes

Guest Name

Messages & Wishes

Guest Name

Memories & Wishes

Guest Name   *Messages & Wishes*

Guest Name

Memories & Wishes

Guest Name

Messages & Wishes

Guest Name

Memories & Wishes

Guest Name

Messages & Wishes

Guest Name   *Memories & Wishes*

_____   _____

                                _____

                                _____

                                _____

_____   _____

                                _____

                                _____

                                _____

_____   _____

                                _____

Guest Name

Messages & Wishes

Guest Name

Memories & Wishes

Guest Name

Messages & Wishes

Guest Name

Memories & Wishes

Guest Name

Messages & Wishes

Guest Name

Memories & Wishes

_____

_____

_____

Guest Name

Messages & Wishes

Guest Name

Memories & Wishes

Guest Name

Messages & Wishes

Guest Name

Memories & Wishes

_____

_____

_____

_____

_____

_____

_____

_____

_____

_____

_____

_____

_____

Guest Name

Messages & Wishes

Guest Name   *Memories & Wishes*

_____   _____

_____   _____

_____   _____

_____   _____

_____   _____

_____

_____

_____

_____

_____

_____

Guest Name

Messages & Wishes

Guest Name

Memories & Wishes

Guest Name

Messages & Wishes

Guest Name

Memories & Wishes

Guest Name

Messages & Wishes

Guest Name

Memories & Wishes

Guest Name

Messages & Wishes

Guest Name

Memories & Wishes

Guest Name

Messages & Wishes

Guest Name

Memories & Wishes

Guest Name

Messages & Wishes

Guest Name

Memories & Wishes

_____

_____

_____

_____

_____

_____

_____

_____

_____

_____

_____

_____

_____

_____

_____

Guest Name

Messages & Wishes

Guest Name

Memories & Wishes

Guest Name

Messages & Wishes

Guest Name

Memories & Wishes

Guest Name

Messages & Wishes

Guest Name

Memories & Wishes

Guest Name

Messages & Wishes

Guest Name

Memories & Wishes

Guest Name

Messages & Wishes

Guest Name

Memories & Wishes

Guest Name

Messages & Wishes

Guest Name

Memories & Wishes

Guest Name

Messages & Wishes

Guest Name

Memories & Wishes

Guest Name

Messages & Wishes

Guest Name

Memories & Wishes

Guest Name

Messages & Wishes

Guest Name

Memories & Wishes

Guest Name

Messages & Wishes

Guest Name

Memories & Wishes

_____

_____

_____

_____

_____

_____

_____

_____

_____

_____

_____

Guest Name

Messages & Wishes

Guest Name

Memories & Wishes

Guest Name

Messages & Wishes

Guest Name

Memories & Wishes

Guest Name

Messages & Wishes

Guest Name

Memories & Wishes

Guest Name

Messages & Wishes

Guest Name

Memories & Wishes

Guest Name

Messages & Wishes

Guest Name

Memories & Wishes

Guest Name

Messages & Wishes

Guest Name

Memories & Wishes

Guest Name

Messages & Wishes

Guest Name

Memories & Wishes

Guest Name

Messages & Wishes

Guest Name

Memories & Wishes

Guest Name

Messages & Wishes

Guest Name   *Memories & Wishes*

Guest Name

Messages & Wishes

Guest Name

Memories & Wishes

Guest Name

Messages & Wishes

Guest Name

Memories & Wishes

Guest Name

Messages & Wishes

Guest Name

Memories & Wishes

Guest Name

Messages & Wishes

Guest Name

Memories & Wishes

Guest Name

Messages & Wishes

_____

_____

_____

Guest Name

Memories & Wishes

Guest Name

Messages & Wishes

Guest Name   Memories & Wishes

Guest Name

Messages & Wishes

Guest Name

Memories & Wishes

Guest Name

Messages & Wishes

Guest Name

Memories & Wishes

Guest Name

Messages & Wishes

Guest Name

Memories & Wishes

_____

_____

_____

Guest Name

Messages & Wishes

Guest Name

Memories & Wishes

_____

_____

_____

Guest Name

Messages & Wishes

_____

_____

_____

_____

_____

_____

_____

_____

_____

_____

_____

_____

Guest Name

Memories & Wishes

Guest Name

Messages & Wishes

_____

_____

_____

_____

_____

_____

_____

_____

_____

_____

_____

Guest Name

Memories & Wishes

Guest Name

Messages & Wishes

Guest Name

Memories & Wishes

Guest Name

Messages & Wishes

Guest Name

Memories & Wishes

Guest Name

Messages & Wishes

Guest Name

Memories & Wishes

Guest Name

Messages & Wishes

Guest Name

Memories & Wishes

Guest Name

Messages & Wishes

Made in the USA
Coppell, TX
13 May 2022

77744140R10070